self-care
CALENDAR
52 weeks

Celeste R. Anderson

This book belongs to:

....

A JOURNEY OF COMPASSION, GROWTH, AND SELF-LOVE

Welcome to "Self-Care Calendar: 52 Weeks of Self-Care," a nurturing guide designed to accompany you on a year-long journey towards holistic well-being. In the following pages, you'll find a sanctuary where your growth, health, and happiness are celebrated and nurtured with gentle care.

This book is more than a collection of activities; it's a canvas for you to paint your own self-care journey. Each week offers a new theme, a new opportunity to explore an aspect of self-care that resonates with your unique life. From the tranquility of mindfulness meditation to the joy of creative expression, each chapter is an invitation to explore, learn, and grow.

Let this book be your companion through the seasons of the year and the seasons of life. It's here to offer comfort on the difficult days, joy on the good ones, and inspiration throughout. Each page is a reminder that you are worthy of care and that taking time for yourself is a beautiful and necessary act of love.

As you turn each page, as you engage with each week's theme, may you find moments of peace, sparks of joy, and a deeper connection with the wonderful person you are. Welcome to your self-care journey.

MAY IT BE A JOURNEY OF LOVE, DISCOVERY, AND PROFOUND FULFILLMENT.

WEEK 1: MINDFULNESS MEDITATION

Embracing Mindfulness Meditation with Heart and Science

Dear reader, welcome to your first step on a transformative journey of self-care. This week, we delve into the world of mindfulness meditation - a gentle, loving practice that offers a sanctuary of calm in our often chaotic lives. Grounded in ancient wisdom, mindfulness meditation has been embraced by modern science for its profound benefits. Research shows it can reduce stress, enhance emotional balance, and improve focus. It's like a warm embrace for your mind, offering solace and clarity in the midst of life's storms.

Simple Steps to Cultivate Mindful Moments

1. Finding Your Space: Choose a quiet, comfortable spot where you can sit undisturbed. This can be a cozy chair, a cushion on the floor, or even a spot in your garden.
2. Embracing the Breath: Begin by focusing on your breath. Feel the air enter through your nostrils, filling your lungs, and then gently leaving your body. This breath is your anchor, your home in the realm of mindfulness.
3. Acknowledging Thoughts: As thoughts arise, greet them with kindness, then let them float away, returning your focus to your breath. It's not about having an empty mind, but about being present with what is.
4. Daily Practice: Aim for 10 minutes of mindfulness meditation each day. You can gradually increase this time as you become more comfortable with the practice.

Reflective Questions

How does my body feel before and after meditation? Notice any physical sensations, tensions, or relaxations.

How does practicing mindfulness affect my daily interactions and feelings? Reflect on any changes in your responses to daily events or emotions.

Weekly Goal

This week, set a gentle, loving goal to practice mindfulness meditation for 10 minutes each day. This is your time, a precious gift you give to yourself, where you can find peace and clarity amidst the hustle of life. Remember, each moment of mindfulness is a step towards a more balanced, serene you.

As you embark on this journey, remember that self-care is a deeply personal and unique experience. Mindfulness meditation is your invitation to pause, breathe, and connect deeply with yourself. Embrace each moment with kindness and curiosity, knowing that each breath is a step towards greater peace and self-understanding. Welcome to a world where each mindful moment is a celebration of your inner journey.

WEEK 2: GRATITUDE JOURNALING

Nurturing Gratitude, Enriching Life

Welcome to Week 2, where we explore the heartwarming practice of gratitude journaling. Embracing gratitude isn't just about feeling good; it's about transforming your perspective on life. Scientific studies have shown that regularly expressing gratitude can enhance mental health, increase happiness, and even improve physical well-being. Gratitude journaling is like planting seeds of positivity that bloom into a garden of inner peace and joy. It's about recognizing and cherishing the abundance of blessings, big and small, that life offers.

Cultivating a Grateful Heart through Journaling

1. Choosing Your Journal: Find a notebook or journal that feels special to you – it can be simple or decorative, whatever resonates with your heart.
2. Dedicated Time: Set aside a few quiet minutes each day for this practice. Early morning or before bedtime are peaceful moments to reflect.
3. Writing with Heart: Each day, write down three things you are grateful for. They can range from significant events to simple joys – a sunny day, a friend's smile, a comforting meal.
4. Depth Over Breadth: Occasionally, choose one item and write in detail about why you're grateful for it. This deepens the experience and fosters a greater appreciation.

Heartfelt Reflections for a Grateful Journey

How does practicing gratitude change my outlook on everyday situations?
Observe any shifts in perception towards daily occurrences or challenges.

In moments of difficulty, how can I find aspects to be grateful for?
Consider the silver linings or lessons in challenging situations.

Weekly Goal

This week, commit to writing in your gratitude journal every day. Let each entry be a loving reminder of the beauty and bounty that life offers. As you pen down your thoughts, allow yourself to fully experience the warmth and joy that gratitude brings. Remember, every note of thanks is a step towards a more contented, fulfilled heart.

As you journey through this week with your gratitude journal, let each word be a gentle embrace of life's gifts. In moments of challenge or routine, pause and find something to be grateful for. This simple act is a powerful tool that can transform your inner world, filling it with love, peace, and a deep sense of fulfillment. Embrace this practice as a loving friend, guiding you to a richer, more vibrant life experience.

WEEK 3: PHYSICAL ACTIVITY

Embracing Movement with Joy and Understanding

Welcome to Week 3, where we celebrate the gift of movement and physical activity. Moving your body is not just about fitness; it's a profound act of self-love and care. Scientifically, regular physical activity boosts your mood, improves sleep, and reduces the risk of chronic diseases. It's like a loving embrace for your body, enhancing not just physical strength but also bringing mental clarity and emotional balance. Each step, stretch, or dance is a way to express gratitude to your body for all it does.

Finding Joy in Movement

1. Discover What You Love: Reflect on physical activities that bring you joy. It could be walking, yoga, dancing, or something entirely different.
2. Set Realistic Goals: Start with achievable goals. If you're new to exercise, begin with 10-15 minutes and gradually increase.
3. Create a Routine: Try to incorporate physical activity into your daily routine. Even short walks or stretching sessions count.
4. Mindful Movement: As you move, focus on how your body feels – the rhythm of your breath, the flow of your movements, and the sensations in your muscles.

Reflecting on the Journey of Physical Wellness

How do I feel emotionally and physically after being active?
Notice changes in mood, energy levels, and bodily sensations.

How does regular physical activity impact my daily life and routines?
Observe any differences in your daily activities, sleep patterns, and overall well-being.

Weekly Goal

Set a goal to engage in physical activity for a certain amount of time each day, tailored to your lifestyle and preferences. Approach this goal with kindness, remembering that each form of movement, no matter how small, is a celebration of your body's capabilities and a step towards better health and happiness.

As you embark on this week of physical activity, remember to treat your body with kindness and respect. There's no need for harsh routines or unrealistic expectations. Find joy in movement, listen to your body's needs, and celebrate each step as a loving gesture towards your well-being. Let this week be a reminder of how movement, in any form, is a powerful act of self-care and love.

WEEK 4: HEALTHY EATING

Nourishing Your Body with Love and Mindfulness

Welcome to Week 4, where we embrace the nurturing practice of healthy eating. <u>This week is not about strict diets or restrictions, but about lovingly fueling your body with what it needs to thrive.</u> Science tells us that healthy eating is more than just food choices; it's about improving overall well-being, boosting energy levels, and enhancing mood. Nutritious foods act as a tender embrace for your body, providing the necessary nutrients for physical health and mental clarity. Each meal is an opportunity to show gratitude to your body for its incredible resilience and strength.

Embarking on a Journey of Mindful Nourishment

1. <u>Understanding Nutrition:</u> Start by learning about basic nutrition - the balance of proteins, carbohydrates, and fats that your body needs.
2. <u>Mindful Eating:</u> Pay attention to what you eat, how it tastes, and how it makes you feel. Savor each bite and eat without distractions.
3. <u>Meal Planning:</u> Plan your meals to include a variety of nutrients. Incorporate colorful fruits and vegetables, whole grains, lean proteins, and healthy fats.
4. <u>Hydration:</u> Remember to hydrate. Water is essential for all bodily functions and helps in maintaining energy levels and concentration.

Contemplating Your Relationship with Food

How does my body feel after eating different types of food?
Notice any changes in energy, digestion, or mood after meals.

How can I make my meals more nourishing and enjoyable?
Think about ways to enhance the nutritional value and pleasure of your meals.

Weekly Goal

This week, aim to mindfully choose at least one meal a day that is balanced and nourishing.
View this as a loving act of self-care, a way to honor your body with the nutrients it needs.
Celebrate the colors, textures, and flavors of your food, and recognize each meal as a step
towards holistic health.

As you journey through this week, remember that healthy eating is a form of self-respect.
It's not about perfection but about making choices that honor your body's needs. Each
mindful meal is a love letter to your body, acknowledging its worth and your commitment
to its care. Embrace this week as an opportunity to strengthen your relationship with food
in a nurturing, compassionate way.

WEEK 5: SLEEP HYGIENE

Embracing Restful Nights with Understanding and Kindness

Welcome to Week 5, a week dedicated to the nurturing practice of sleep hygiene. Sleep, dear reader, is not just a physical necessity but a loving embrace for your mind and body. It's during these restful hours that healing and rejuvenation occur. <u>Science illuminates the importance of quality sleep for emotional regulation, cognitive function, and overall health</u>. By cultivating good sleep hygiene, you're not just resting your body; you're nourishing your soul, allowing yourself to wake up to a world of renewed possibilities and energy.

Gentle Steps Towards Peaceful Slumber

1. <u>Creating a Restful Environment:</u> Make your bedroom a sanctuary for sleep. Ensure it's dark, quiet, and cool. Consider soothing colors and comfortable bedding.
2. <u>Establishing a Relaxing Bedtime Routine:</u> Develop calming pre-sleep rituals like reading, gentle stretching, or listening to soft music. This signals to your body that it's time to wind down.
3. <u>Mindful of Meals and Caffeine:</u> Avoid heavy meals, caffeine, and alcohol close to bedtime, as they can disrupt sleep.
4. <u>Consistent Sleep Schedule:</u> Try to go to bed and wake up at the same time every day, even on weekends, to regulate your body's internal clock.

Contemplating Your Sleep Journey

How do I feel after a night of good versus poor sleep?
Notice the difference in your energy, mood, and mental clarity.

How does my daytime routine influence my sleep?
Consider how factors like physical activity and screen time affect your sleep.

Weekly Goal

Your goal this week is to implement one or two changes that promote better sleep hygiene. Whether it's adjusting your sleeping environment, establishing a bedtime routine, or being mindful of your evening diet, treat each change as a gentle gift to yourself. Recognize the value of rest and honor your need for it, as every night of good sleep is a step towards a healthier, happier you.

As you move through this week, remember that sleep is a form of self-love. It's a time for your body and mind to heal, reset, and prepare for the new day ahead. Embrace this practice with kindness and patience, knowing that each night is an opportunity to care for yourself in the most fundamental and nurturing way. Sweet dreams, dear reader.

WEEK 6: DIGITAL DETOX

Reconnecting with Yourself and the World Beyond Screens

Welcome to Week 6, where we gently explore the concept of a digital detox. In our fast-paced, connected world, it's easy to forget the joy of simply being present. A digital detox is not about shunning technology but about finding balance and reconnecting with the non-digital aspects of life. Research shows that excessive screen time can impact mental health, sleep patterns, and even personal relationships. By mindfully reducing our digital consumption, we create space for deeper connections with ourselves and the world around us, embracing a sense of peace and presence often lost in the digital noise.

Mindful Steps to Unplug and Recharge

1. Awareness of Screen Time: Start by becoming aware of how much time you spend on digital devices. What are you engaging with, and how does it make you feel?
2. Setting Boundaries: Allocate specific times for checking emails, social media, and other digital platforms. Outside these times, try to stay offline.
3. Tech-Free Zones: Create areas in your home, like the bedroom or dining area, where digital devices are not allowed.
4. Engaging in Non-Digital Activities: Rediscover hobbies and activities that don't involve screens – reading, painting, gardening, or simply enjoying nature.

Contemplating Your Digital Habits

How do I feel emotionally and physically after a period away from digital devices?
Notice any changes in your stress levels, mood, and bodily sensations.

How do my digital habits impact my relationships and daily life?
Think about the influence of screen time on your interactions and presence with others.

Weekly Goal

Your gentle goal for this week is to consciously reduce your screen time each day. Whether it's an hour less than usual or specific tech-free periods, view this as a loving commitment to your well-being. Embrace the freedom and peace that come with disconnecting, allowing yourself to reconnect with life's simple, beautiful moments.

As you journey through this week's digital detox, remember that technology is a tool to enhance life, not to overshadow it. Reconnect with the world around you, the people you love, and most importantly, with yourself. Each moment spent away from the screen is an opportunity to nurture your mind, body, and spirit in the most loving and present way.

WEEK 7: NATURE CONNECTION

Embracing the Healing Embrace of Nature

Welcome to Week 7, where we step into the nurturing arms of nature. This week is about reconnecting with the earth and finding tranquility in its embrace. <u>Science supports the profound impact of nature on our well-being. Being in natural surroundings can lower stress, enhance mood, and improve overall health.</u> It's a gentle reminder of the world's beauty and our place within it. In nature, we find a peaceful retreat from the hustle of daily life, a place where we can breathe deeply, ground ourselves, and rejuvenate our spirits.

Finding Solace and Joy in the Natural World

1. <u>Daily Nature Moments:</u> Dedicate time each day to be outside. It could be a morning walk, a break in a nearby park, or simply enjoying a sunset.
2. <u>Sensory Connection:</u> While in nature, engage all your senses. Notice the sounds of birds, the scent of the trees, the feel of the breeze, and the beauty around you.
3. <u>Nature Journaling:</u> Keep a journal to record your experiences in nature. You can write, sketch, or even press leaves and flowers.
4. <u>Eco-Friendly Practices:</u> Cultivate a deeper relationship with nature by adopting eco-friendly habits, like recycling or using reusable products.

Deepening Your Connection with Nature

How does spending time in nature affect my mental and emotional state?
Observe any changes in your stress levels, thoughts, and emotions.

How can I integrate the peace of nature into my daily life?
Think of ways to bring elements of nature into your home or routine.

Weekly Goal

Your goal for this week is to consciously spend time in nature each day. Whether it's a short walk, sitting in a garden, or simply observing the sky from your window, let these moments be a loving practice of self-care. Embrace the beauty and serenity of the natural world, allowing it to refresh and invigorate your soul.

As you explore your connection with nature this week, remember that you are part of this magnificent tapestry of life. Each tree, bird, and breeze is a reminder of the earth's endless generosity and beauty. Let nature's wisdom guide you to a place of peace and grounding, nurturing your heart with its gentle, healing touch.

WEEK 8: CREATIVE EXPRESSION

date:

Celebrating Your Inner World through Creativity

Welcome to Week 8, a week dedicated to the joy and liberation found in creative expression. This week, we invite you to explore the endless possibilities of your imagination. Engaging in creative activities isn't just about producing something; it's a form of self-expression, a way to communicate what's within you in a language beyond words. <u>Science reveals that creative expression can reduce stress, improve mental health, and bring a sense of accomplishment and happiness.</u> It's a way to embrace your inner self, to play, explore, and express freely - an act of self-love and understanding.

Unleashing Your Creative Spirit

1. <u>Exploring Different Mediums:</u> Try various forms of creative expression - drawing, painting, writing, music, dance, or crafting. See which medium speaks to your soul.
2. <u>Daily Creative Time:</u> Set aside a small amount of time each day for creative activities. Even 10-15 minutes can spark joy and inspiration.
3. <u>Creating Without Judgment:</u> Approach your creative time with an open mind. It's not about perfection but about the process and experience.
4. <u>Inspiration in the Everyday:</u> Find inspiration in your daily life. Nature, music, conversations, and personal experiences can all ignite creative ideas.

Nurturing Your Creative Journey

How do I feel when I'm engaged in creative activities?
Notice the emotions and thoughts that arise during your creative process.

How does creative expression enrich my life?
Think about the impact of creativity on your overall well-being and happiness.

Weekly Goal

Set a goal to engage in at least one creative activity each day this week. Let this be a time of exploration and self-discovery, a sacred space where you can express your thoughts, feelings, and dreams. Remember, each act of creativity is a celebration of your unique inner world, a loving gesture towards yourself.

As you immerse yourself in creative expression this week, let go of any expectations or judgments. Allow yourself to play, explore, and create from a place of joy and authenticity. This is your time to honor your creativity, to listen to your heart, and to express all the beauty that lies within you. Embrace this journey with love and openness, and watch as your creative spirit flourishes.

WEEK 9: SOCIAL CONNECTIONS

date:

Nurturing the Heart through Meaningful Connections

Welcome to Week 9, a week dedicated to the warmth and fulfillment found in social connections. <u>In this week, we focus on the beauty of human relationships and the joy of sharing our journey with others.</u> The science of connection tells us that meaningful relationships are vital for our emotional well-being. They provide support, joy, and a sense of belonging. In a world often rushed and individualistic, taking time to foster connections is a profound act of self-care and love. It's about building bridges of understanding, compassion, and companionship in our shared human experience.

Cultivating Connections with Kindness and Presence

1. <u>Reaching Out:</u> Make an effort to connect with friends or family. This could be a phone call, a message, or planning a meet-up.
2. <u>Listening with Empathy:</u> Engage in conversations where you actively listen, offering your full attention and empathy.
3. <u>Joining Community Activities:</u> Participate in local events or groups that align with your interests, providing an opportunity to meet like-minded individuals.
4. <u>Expressing Gratitude:</u> Show appreciation for the people in your life. A simple thank you, a note, or a small gesture can deepen connections.

Exploring the Depth of Your Social World

How do social interactions impact my mood and outlook?
Observe the emotional and mental changes following social engagements.

How can I be more present and authentic in my interactions?
Consider ways to be more engaged and genuine in your social connections.

Weekly Goal

Your goal this week is to actively nurture your social connections. Aim to initiate or deepen at least one meaningful interaction each day. Whether it's a conversation, a shared activity, or simply being there for someone, let each interaction be a heartfelt expression of your desire to connect.

As you journey through this week, remember the power of human connection in nurturing your soul. Each interaction is an opportunity to give and receive love, to understand and be understood, and to share in the beautiful tapestry of human experience. Approach your connections with openness, kindness, and the intention to build bridges of empathy and understanding. In doing so, you're not only enriching your life but also bringing light and warmth into the lives of others.

WEEK 10: PERSONAL SPACE ORGANIZATION

date:

Creating Harmony in Your Personal Space

Welcome to Week 10, where we lovingly embrace the art of organizing our personal spaces. This week is about more than just tidying up; it's about creating an environment that reflects and supports your inner peace and well-being. Research has shown that the state of our physical spaces can greatly impact our mental health. A cluttered space can lead to a cluttered mind, increasing stress and reducing productivity. By mindfully organizing your surroundings, you are caring for your mental and emotional health, creating a sanctuary that nurtures calmness, clarity, and joy.

Harmonizing Your Environment with Care

1. Decluttering with Purpose: Begin by choosing one area to declutter. It could be a desk, a closet, or any space that feels overwhelming.
2. Mindful Sorting: As you sort through items, ask yourself if each item brings value or joy. If not, consider donating or recycling it.
3. Organizing with Love: Once you've decluttered, organize the remaining items in a way that makes the space feel open, peaceful, and functional.
4. Personalizing Your Space: Add elements that bring you joy – this could be plants, photographs, or a piece of art that uplifts your spirit.

Contemplating Your Relationship with Your Space

How does the state of my space affect my mood and productivity?
Notice the emotional and mental changes that come with different levels of organization.

How can my space better reflect and support my well-being?
Think about ways your environment can become a true reflection of your inner peace and joy.

Weekly Goal

Set a goal this week to organize and personalize one area of your space. Approach this task not as a chore, but as a loving act of self-care. Recognize that each step in organizing your environment is a step towards a more peaceful and harmonious inner world.

As you engage in the process of organizing your space this week, remember to do so with kindness and patience. Your surroundings are an extension of your inner self. By caring for your space, you are also caring for your mind and heart. Let this practice be a gentle journey towards creating a sanctuary that resonates with tranquility, clarity, and joy – a space where you can thrive, dream, and find peace.

WEEK 11: SELF-COMPASSION

date:

Embracing Yourself with Kindness and Understanding

Welcome to Week 11, a week dedicated to the gentle practice of self-compassion. This week, we turn our focus inward, to the way we treat and perceive ourselves. Self-compassion is about being as kind and understanding to ourselves as we would be to a dear friend. Research in psychology shows that practicing self-compassion leads to greater emotional resilience, reduces anxiety and depression, and helps us recover more quickly from setbacks. It's about acknowledging our imperfections, not as faults, but as part of the shared human experience, and treating ourselves with kindness and grace.

Nurturing a Compassionate Relationship with Yourself

1. Mindful Acknowledgment: Notice when you're being self-critical. Pause and acknowledge these thoughts without judgment.
2. Self-Compassion Break: When you notice self-criticism, take a moment to comfort yourself. Place a hand over your heart and offer yourself some kind words.
3. Gratitude for Yourself: Each day, think of three things you appreciate about yourself. These can be qualities, actions, or simply your ability to endure tough times.
4. Compassionate Letter to Self: Write a letter to yourself from the perspective of a loving friend. Address your challenges and offer kindness and understanding.

Exploring Your Inner Compassionate Voice

How do I talk to myself when I make mistakes or face challenges?
Reflect on the tone and content of your self-talk during difficult moments.

How does practicing self-compassion affect my overall well-being?
Notice any changes in your mood, stress levels, and interactions with others.

Weekly Goal

Your goal for this week is to practice self-compassion daily. <u>Whether it's through mindful acknowledgment, self-compassion breaks, or gratitude, let each act be a gentle reminder of your worthiness and humanity.</u> Recognize that you deserve the same kindness and care that you so readily give to others.

As you move through this week, hold yourself in a space of love and patience. <u>Remember, being compassionate towards yourself is not a sign of weakness, but a courageous act of acknowledging and embracing your true self, with all its strengths and vulnerabilities.</u> Let this week be a turning point in how you relate to yourself, marking the beginning of a more loving, understanding, and compassionate journey within.

WEEK 12: STRESS MANAGEMENT

date:

Embracing Calm in the Midst of Life's Storms

Welcome to Week 12, a week devoted to the nurturing practice of stress management. In our often hectic and demanding lives, stress can seem like a constant companion. However, managing stress is crucial for our overall well-being. <u>Scientific research has shown that effective stress management can lead to improved mental health, better physical health, and increased life satisfaction.</u> This week, we focus on recognizing stress and gently guiding ourselves back to a state of calm and balance. It's about understanding that while stress is a part of life, it doesn't have to control it.

Gentle Steps Towards Peace and Balance

1. <u>Identifying Stressors:</u> Start by recognizing what triggers your stress. Is it work, relationships, health, or something else?
2. <u>Breathing Exercises:</u> When you feel stressed, take a few minutes to focus on your breath. Deep, slow breathing can help calm your mind and body.
3. <u>Mindful Movement:</u> Engage in gentle physical activities like walking, yoga, or stretching to release the tension in your body.
4. <u>Setting Boundaries:</u> Learn to say no and set healthy boundaries in your life. Recognize that it's okay to prioritize your well-being.

Understanding Your Personal Stress Landscape

How does stress manifest in my body and mind?
Notice any physical sensations or thoughts that arise when you're stressed.

How can I introduce more calming practices into my daily routine?
Think of ways to incorporate stress-reducing activities into your day.

Weekly Goal

<u>Your goal this week is to consciously apply stress management techniques each day</u>. Whether it's through breathing exercises, setting boundaries, or mindful movement, approach these practices with kindness and patience. Remember, each step you take towards managing stress is an act of love and care for yourself.

As you explore stress management this week, be gentle with yourself. Recognize that stress is a natural response, but you have the power to soothe and comfort yourself in these moments. Embrace each stress-reducing practice as a precious gift to your mind, body, and spirit, allowing yourself to find peace and balance in the midst of life's challenges.

WEEK 13: POSITIVE AFFIRMATIONS

Cultivating a Garden of Positivity in Your Mind

Welcome to Week 13, where we embrace the nurturing practice of positive affirmations. In this week, we focus on the power of words and thoughts in shaping our reality. Positive affirmations are not just feel-good quotes; they are a way to rewire our brains. Science shows that regularly practicing positive affirmations can significantly impact our thinking patterns, leading to a more optimistic outlook, increased self-esteem, and a greater sense of well-being. By affirming our strengths and values, we plant seeds of positivity and growth in the fertile soil of our minds.

Sowing Seeds of Positivity Through Affirmations

1. Creating Personal Affirmations: Reflect on areas where you seek growth or support. Craft affirmations that resonate with your goals and aspirations.
2. Daily Affirmation Practice: Set aside time each morning or evening to repeat your affirmations. Say them out loud, write them down, or meditate on them.
3. Affirmation Reminders: Place your affirmations where you can see them regularly – on your mirror, as a phone wallpaper, or on a desk note.
4. Affirmation Reflection: At the end of the day, reflect on how your affirmations made you feel and how they influenced your thoughts and actions.

Exploring the Impact of Positive Self-Talk

How do my affirmations influence my mood and self-perception?
Notice any shifts in how you feel about yourself throughout the day.

How can I make my affirmations more meaningful and powerful to me?
Think about ways to personalize your affirmations so they deeply resonate with you.

Weekly Goal

Your goal this week is to consistently practice your chosen affirmations each day. Let these affirmations be a loving reminder of your strengths, capabilities, and worth. Embrace them as tools for transformation and self-empowerment.

As you engage in this practice, remember that each positive statement is a step towards nurturing a more loving and supportive relationship with yourself. Positive affirmations are like rays of light, illuminating the beauty and potential within you. Allow them to guide you towards a mindset filled with hope, strength, and self-compassion.

WEEK 14: READING FOR PLEASURE

Embarking on Literary Journeys of Discovery and Joy

Welcome to Week 14, where we celebrate the joy of reading for pleasure. In the pages of a book, we find gateways to other worlds, insights into different perspectives, and a respite from the hustle of everyday life. <u>Reading is not just an escape; it's a journey of exploration and growth.</u> Scientific studies highlight the benefits of reading for pleasure, including reduced stress levels, improved empathy, and enhanced mental agility. This week, we invite you to immerse yourself in the enriching world of literature, allowing stories and ideas to soothe, inspire, and rejuvenate your spirit.

Nurturing Your Mind and Soul Through Reading

1. <u>Choosing Your Reading Material:</u> Select a book that sparks your interest. It could be fiction, non-fiction, poetry, or even graphic novels.
2. <u>Creating a Reading Ritual:</u> Find a comfortable, quiet spot for reading. Maybe it's a cozy chair with a cup of tea or a sunny spot in the park.
3. <u>Setting Aside Time for Reading:</u> Dedicate a specific time each day for reading, even if it's just for a few minutes.
4. <u>Reading Without Pressure:</u> Remember, the goal is enjoyment. There's no pressure to finish a certain number of pages or books.

Exploring the Impact of Reading on Your Well-being

How do I feel during and after reading?
Notice any changes in your stress levels, mood, and thoughts.

How does reading enrich my understanding of the world and myself?
Consider how the perspectives and experiences in your reading material contribute to your personal growth.

Weekly Goal

Set a goal this week to engage in reading for pleasure each day. Let this be a time of relaxation, curiosity, and personal discovery. Approach your reading as a gentle journey into the vast and wonderful world of stories and ideas.

As you delve into your chosen reading material this week, allow yourself to be transported by the magic of words. Let each book, each story, be a loving invitation to explore, dream, and reflect. Remember, in the realm of books, you're not just reading; you're embarking on a journey of the heart and mind, one that nourishes and enriches your soul in every page.

WEEK 15: ART APPRECIATION

Embracing the Beauty and Soul of Art

Welcome to Week 15, a week dedicated to the joy and enrichment of art appreciation. Art, in its myriad forms, is not just a visual experience but a journey into the depths of human emotion and creativity. Engaging with art allows us to explore new perspectives, experience a range of emotions, and connect with our inner selves. Scientific research has shown that appreciating art can reduce stress, increase empathy, and enhance critical thinking skills. This week, we invite you to open your heart to the beauty of art, allowing it to inspire, challenge, and move you in profound ways.

Discovering the World Through Art

1. Exploring Different Art Forms: Delve into various types of art - paintings, sculptures, photography, or digital art. Explore different styles and periods.
2. Visiting Art Virtually or In-Person: Plan a visit to an art gallery, museum, or explore online art collections. Take your time to really look at and appreciate the artworks.
3. Reflecting on Art: After viewing an artwork, spend some time reflecting on how it makes you feel. What emotions, thoughts, or memories does it evoke?
4. Artistic Expression at Home: Create an art-inspired space in your home, whether it's hanging a print of a favorite artwork or arranging space in a way that reflects a certain artistic style.

Deepening Your Connection with Art

How does engaging with art affect my emotional state?
Notice any feelings or moods that arise when you view different artworks.

Think about how the creativity and beauty of art can be reflected in your everyday activities and surroundings.

Weekly Goal

<u>Set a goal this week to explore and appreciate art in some form each day.</u> Whether it's a short visit to a gallery, an online art exploration, or simply enjoying an artwork in your home, let each experience be a step towards a deeper appreciation of the beauty and diversity of human expression.

As you immerse yourself in the world of art this week, <u>allow yourself to be moved, challenged, and inspired.</u> Art is a conversation between the creator and the observer, a dialogue that spans time and space. Embrace this opportunity to connect with this dialogue, letting the language of art speak to your heart and soul.

WEEK 16: LEARNING A NEW SKILL

Embarking on a Journey of Growth and Discovery

Welcome to Week 16, a time to celebrate the joy and fulfillment that comes from learning a new skill. This week is about more than just acquiring knowledge; it's about embracing growth, challenging ourselves, and enriching our lives. Engaging in continuous learning has been shown by research to keep our minds active and sharp, boost our confidence, and open up new opportunities and perspectives. Whether it's a practical skill, a creative pursuit, or intellectual exploration, learning something new is a profound act of self-care – a testament to our never-ending potential for growth and development.

Nurturing Your Mind and Spirit through Learning

1. Choosing a Skill: Select a skill you've always wanted to learn or are curious about. It could be a new language, a musical instrument, cooking a specific cuisine, or anything that sparks your interest.
2. Setting Realistic Goals: Break down the learning process into small, manageable goals. Celebrate each small step of progress.
3. Creating a Learning Schedule: Dedicate regular time in your routine for this new learning. Consistency is key.
4. Engaging with Learning Resources: Utilize books, online courses, videos, or local classes to help you learn. Be open to different methods of learning.

Contemplating Your Learning Journey

How does learning this new skill make me feel?
Notice any feelings of excitement, challenge, frustration, or accomplishment.

Consider the ways in which this learning experience is adding value to your daily routine or long-term goals.

Weekly Goal

Your goal this week is to dedicate time each day to your chosen skill. Approach this learning experience with curiosity and patience, recognizing that every challenge is an opportunity for growth. Let this new skill be a source of joy, self-discovery, and personal fulfillment.

As you embark on this journey of learning, remember that it's about the process, not just the outcome. Each step in this journey is a celebration of your capacity to grow and evolve. Be gentle with yourself, embrace the challenges, and relish the journey of becoming more than you were yesterday. Learning a new skill is not just about acquiring knowledge; it's about enriching your life and nurturing your soul.

WEEK 17: MINDFUL COOKING

Savoring the Moment in the Kitchen with Heart and Soul

Welcome to Week 17, where we explore the nurturing art of mindful cooking. This week is about transforming our daily cooking routine into a meditative and joyful practice. Mindful cooking is more than just preparing food; it's an act of love and presence. It allows us to connect with the ingredients, the process, and the moment. <u>Scientific research has shown that engaging in mindful activities, like cooking, can reduce stress, enhance well-being, and bring a sense of accomplishment and creativity.</u> This week, we invite you to experience the kitchen as a sanctuary where each chop, stir, and simmer is an opportunity to be present and to nourish both body and soul.

Creating Culinary Magic with Mindfulness

1. <u>Choosing Your Ingredients Mindfully:</u> Take the time to select your ingredients thoughtfully. Consider their sources, the nourishment they provide, and their flavors and textures.
2. <u>Engaging All Your Senses:</u> As you cook, fully engage your senses. Notice the colors of the ingredients, the sounds of cooking, the aromas, and the textures.
3. <u>Cooking with Intention:</u> Approach each step of the cooking process with intention and focus. Be present with the task at hand, whether it's chopping vegetables or stirring a sauce.
4. <u>Savoring Your Creation:</u> When it's time to eat, do so mindfully. Appreciate the flavors and the effort that went into creating the meal.

Feeding Your Body and Soul Through Cooking

How does mindful cooking affect my mood and stress levels?
Notice any changes in your emotions or stress when you are cooking mindfully.

Think about ways to regularly integrate mindful practices into your cooking.

Weekly Goal

Your goal this week is to practice mindful cooking each day. View this time as an opportunity to connect with the present moment, to express creativity, and to nurture yourself and your loved ones. Allow the act of cooking to be a source of relaxation and joy.

As you engage in mindful cooking this week, remember that every ingredient, every movement, is part of a beautiful dance of nourishment and care. Let the kitchen be a place where you can find calm, express creativity, and celebrate the simple joys of life. Each meal you prepare is not just food; it's a manifestation of love, care, and presence.

WEEK 18: FINANCIAL WELLNESS

date:

Cultivating Peace of Mind through Financial Wellness

Welcome to Week 18, a week dedicated to nurturing your financial wellness. <u>This aspect of self-care is often overlooked, yet it plays a crucial role in our overall well-being.</u> Financial wellness is not about wealth or affluence; it's about creating a sense of security and peace of mind. <u>Research shows that financial stress can significantly impact mental health, relationships, and quality of life.</u> This week, we gently explore ways to bring more clarity, mindfulness, and intentionality to your financial life, helping to alleviate stress and create a foundation of stability and peace.

Fostering Financial Health with Kindness and Practicality

1. <u>Understanding Your Financial Picture:</u> Begin by getting a clear view of your finances. This includes income, expenses, debts, and savings.
2. <u>Budgeting with Compassion:</u> Create a budget that allows you to meet your needs, save for the future, but also enjoy the present. Remember, budgeting is not about restriction, but about making mindful decisions.
3. <u>Setting Financial Goals:</u> Identify short-term and long-term financial goals. These should be realistic, achievable, and aligned with your values and aspirations.
4. <u>Educating Yourself:</u> Spend some time each week learning about financial management. This could be reading articles, books, or even attending a workshop.

Exploring Your Relationship with Money

How does my financial situation affect my emotional well-being?
Notice any stress, anxiety, or peace of mind related to your finances.

How can I improve my financial wellness in a way that feels caring and sustainable?

Weekly Goal

Set a goal this week to actively engage in one aspect of financial wellness. Whether it's creating a budget, setting a financial goal, or educating yourself about money management, approach this with a sense of care and purpose. Remember, taking steps towards financial wellness is an act of self-love and a commitment to your peace of mind.

As you navigate this week, hold your financial wellness journey with compassion and understanding. Financial matters can be complex and emotionally charged, but approaching them with mindfulness and intention can bring a sense of control and tranquility. Let this week be a step towards creating a more balanced, peaceful financial life, aligned with your values and goals.

WEEK 19: YOGA AND FLEXIBILITY

date:

Embracing the Harmonious Balance of Yoga

Welcome to Week 19, a week dedicated to the gentle art of yoga and the nurturing practice of flexibility. Yoga is much more than physical exercise; it's a holistic practice that unites the body, mind, and spirit. Engaging in yoga brings numerous benefits, as supported by scientific research, including reduced stress, improved mental clarity, enhanced physical strength, and increased flexibility. This week, we invite you to explore yoga as a form of self-care, a pathway to inner peace and harmony. It's about moving your body with love, respecting its limits, and gradually expanding its capabilities.

Nurturing Body and Mind Through Yoga

1. Finding a Yoga Practice: Choose a style of yoga that resonates with you. It could be a gentle, restorative yoga or something more dynamic like Vinyasa. There are plenty of online classes for beginners.
2. Creating a Yoga Space: Set up a comfortable space for your practice. It could be a quiet corner with a yoga mat and perhaps a candle or some calming music.
3. Regular Practice: Try to incorporate a short yoga session into your daily routine. Even 10-15 minutes can make a significant difference.
4. Mindful Movement: As you move through each pose, focus on your breath and how your body feels. Be present in each moment and movement.

Deepening Your Yoga Journey

How does my body feel during and after yoga?
Notice any sensations of stretching, release, or areas of tension and ease.

Think about how the mindfulness, balance, and calm of yoga can be applied to other areas of your life.

Weekly Goal

Your goal this week is to engage in yoga practice regularly, honoring your body's limits and needs. Let each session be an exploration of self-awareness and self-care, a time to connect deeply with your inner self. Remember, yoga is not about perfection but about growth, balance, and finding peace within.

As you journey through this week with yoga, embrace each pose with compassion and mindfulness. Allow yoga to be a gentle guide to understanding your body and mind more deeply. Each stretch, each breath is an opportunity to cultivate flexibility, strength, and tranquility, not just physically, but in all aspects of your being.

WEEK 20: AROMATHERAPY AND RELAXATION

date:

Soothing the Senses with the Art of Aromatherapy

Welcome to Week 20, a time to explore the gentle and nurturing world of aromatherapy and relaxation. Aromatherapy, the practice of using natural plant essences to promote health and well-being, has been embraced for its ability to soothe the mind, uplift the spirit, and create a sense of balance and harmony. <u>Scientific studies have shown that certain scents can significantly impact our mood, stress levels, and even sleep quality.</u> This week, we invite you to immerse yourself in the world of aromas, allowing them to guide you to a place of deeper relaxation and peace.

Embracing Tranquility Through Scents

1. <u>Exploring Essential Oils:</u> Start by exploring different essential oils. Common relaxing scents include lavender, chamomile, rose, and sandalwood.
2. <u>Creating a Relaxing Atmosphere:</u> Use a diffuser to disperse your chosen essential oil in your living space, or add a few drops to a warm bath.
3. <u>Mindful Inhalation:</u> Take moments throughout your day for mindful inhalation. Place a drop of essential oil on a tissue and take a few deep, gentle breaths.
4. <u>Scented Bedtime Ritual:</u> Incorporate aromatherapy into your bedtime routine to enhance sleep quality. Lavender oil, for instance, can be applied to pillowcases or used in a bedside diffuser.

Exploring the Impact of Aromatherapy on Well-being

How do different scents affect my mood and stress levels?
Notice any changes in your emotions or relaxation levels when you experience certain aromas.

How can I incorporate aromatherapy into my daily self-care routine?

Weekly Goal

Your goal for this week is to incorporate aromatherapy into your daily routine. Whether it's through a diffuser, a scented bath, or mindful inhalation, let each aromatic experience be an act of self-care and relaxation. Embrace the power of scents to bring calmness and joy into your moments.

As you explore aromatherapy this week, allow the fragrances to be gentle messengers of peace and comfort. Let each scent envelop you in a loving embrace, reminding you of the beauty and serenity that life offers. Aromatherapy is not just about pleasant smells; it's a pathway to inner tranquility, a harmonious dance of the senses that nurtures the soul.

WEEK 21: JOURNAL WRITING

date:

Embracing the Healing Power of Journal Writing

Welcome to Week 21, where we delve into the introspective and nurturing practice of journal writing. Journaling is more than just a method of recording events; it's a powerful tool for self-exploration, emotional expression, and personal growth. Scientific studies have shown that journaling can significantly improve mental health by providing an outlet for expressing thoughts and feelings, reducing stress, and enhancing self-awareness. This week, we encourage you to embrace journal writing as a form of self-care, a sacred space where you can freely express your innermost thoughts, reflect on your experiences, and connect with your true self.

Nurturing Your Inner World Through Journaling

1. Choosing a Journal: Select a journal that resonates with you – it might be a simple notebook, a beautifully bound book, or even a digital journal.
2. Creating a Journaling Ritual: Find a quiet, comfortable space for your journaling. Set aside a regular time each day, even if it's just for a few minutes.
3. Writing Freely: Write without censoring yourself. Let your thoughts and feelings flow onto the page. Remember, this journal is a private space for you.
4. Exploring Different Journaling Techniques: Try various journaling methods such as gratitude journaling, stream of consciousness writing, or reflective journaling on specific questions or themes.

Deepening Your Journaling Experience

How does journaling affect my emotional and mental state?
Notice any shifts in your mood, stress levels, or clarity of thought after journaling.

How can I use journaling to support my goals and aspirations?

Weekly Goal

Set a goal to engage in journal writing each day this week. Let this practice be a nurturing journey of self-discovery and expression. Approach each journaling session with an open heart, allowing it to be a source of comfort, insight, and personal growth.

As you embark on your journaling journey this week, treat each entry as a step towards deeper self-understanding and self-compassion. Your journal is a safe space where you can explore your thoughts and emotions without judgment. Embrace this practice as a loving conversation with yourself, a chance to listen to your inner voice and honor your personal story.

WEEK 22: CULTIVATING PATIENCE

Embracing the Gentle Art of Patience

Welcome to Week 22, a time to nurture the virtue of patience within ourselves. In our fast-paced world, patience is often overlooked, yet it's a powerful form of self-care. Cultivating patience is about more than just waiting calmly; it's about developing a sense of peace and resilience in the face of life's challenges. Scientific research has shown that patience can lead to better mental health, reduce stress levels, and improve decision-making. This week, we invite you to explore patience as a path to inner tranquility and understanding, a way to gracefully navigate the ebb and flow of life.

Fostering Patience in Everyday Life

1. Mindful Observation: Practice observing situations without immediate reaction. Whether it's a slow line at the store or a traffic jam, use this time for mindful breathing and observation.
2. Setting Realistic Expectations: Adjust your expectations in situations where delays or challenges are possible. Remind yourself that some things take time.
3. Reflecting Before Responding: When feeling impatient, take a moment to pause and breathe deeply before responding to the situation.
4. Patience Affirmations: Create affirmations that reinforce patience. For example, "I am calm and patient in all situations" or "I embrace life's pace with tranquility."

Exploring the Role of Patience in Your Life

How do I typically react in situations that test my patience?
Reflect on your responses and what they reveal about your relationship with patience.

How can developing patience improve my daily experiences?

Weekly Goal

Your goal for this week is to consciously practice patience in situations where you might typically feel rushed or frustrated. View each of these moments as an opportunity to cultivate a sense of calm and presence. Remember, patience is a form of self-compassion and understanding, a gift you give to yourself and those around you.

As you focus on cultivating patience this week, embrace each moment with a gentle and open heart. Let patience be a soothing balm for the hurried moments of life, a reminder of the strength and peace that reside within you. Each step towards greater patience is a step towards a more harmonious and fulfilling life.

WEEK 23: EXPLORING MUSIC

Harmonizing Life with the Melody of Music

Welcome to Week 23, where we immerse ourselves in the beautiful world of music. Music is not just a series of notes and rhythms; it's a profound language that speaks directly to our hearts and souls. Engaging with music can be incredibly therapeutic, offering emotional release, relaxation, and joy. <u>Scientific research has shown that music can significantly impact our mental health, reducing stress and anxiety while enhancing overall well-being.</u> This week, we invite you to explore music in all its forms, letting it touch and enrich your life in new and profound ways.

Embracing the Healing Power of Music

1. <u>Diverse Music Exploration:</u> Each day, listen to a different genre or style of music. This could range from classical to jazz, folk to rock, or world music.
2. <u>Mindful Listening:</u> Spend time listening to music mindfully. Focus on the lyrics, the melody, the instruments, and notice how it makes you feel.
3. <u>Music and Movement:</u> Allow music to inspire movement. Dance freely to your favorite tunes, letting the rhythm guide your body.
4. <u>Creating Playlists:</u> Create playlists for different moods or activities - a calming playlist for relaxation, an uplifting playlist for motivation, etc.

Discovering Your Musical Journey

How does different music affect my emotions and mood?
Notice the emotional responses you have to various types of music.

How can music be integrated into my daily routine for wellness?

Weekly Goal

Set a goal to integrate music into your life each day this week. Whether it's active listening, dancing, or creating playlists, let each musical experience be an act of self-care. Embrace the power of music to soothe, energize, and inspire you.

As you explore the world of music this week, let each note, each melody, be a gentle caress for your soul. Allow music to be a companion in your moments of joy, solace in times of sorrow, and a source of inspiration and connection. Music has the unique ability to transcend words, touching the deepest parts of our being. Let it guide you to a place of deeper understanding, harmony, and peace.

WEEK 24: WATER INTAKE AND HYDRATION

Nourishing Your Body with the Essence of Life - Water

Welcome to Week 24, where we focus on the simple yet profound act of hydrating our bodies. Water is the foundation of life, an essential component of our physical well-being. Staying well-hydrated is crucial for maintaining health, as it affects every cell and system in our bodies. <u>Scientific studies have shown that proper hydration can improve mood, enhance brain function, and boost energy levels.</u> This week, we invite you to mindfully focus on your water intake, treating each sip as an act of self-love and appreciation for your body's incredible functions.

Embracing the Habit of Hydration

1. <u>Monitoring Your Water Intake:</u> Keep track of how much water you drink each day. Aim for the recommended amount, usually around 8-10 glasses, but remember this can vary based on individual needs and activity levels.
2. <u>Infusing Flavor:</u> If plain water doesn't appeal to you, try infusing it with fruits, cucumbers, or herbs for a refreshing twist.
3. <u>Setting Hydration Reminders:</u> Use reminders on your phone or notes around your workspace to prompt regular sips throughout the day.
4. <u>Hydrating Foods:</u> Incorporate water-rich foods into your diet, such as cucumbers, lettuce, watermelon, and oranges, to boost your hydration.

Exploring the Impact of Hydration on Well-being

How does my body feel when I'm properly hydrated compared to when I'm not?
Notice any differences in energy levels, mental clarity, and overall physical sensations.

Observe any changes in your mood, concentration, and cognitive abilities when you increase your water intake.

Weekly Goal

Your goal for this week is to consciously maintain a healthy level of hydration each day. View this practice as a nurturing gesture towards your body, honoring its needs and the vital role water plays in your health and well-being.

As you focus on hydration this week, remember that each glass of water is a gift to your body, a necessary element for its optimal functioning. Hydration is a simple yet powerful form of self-care, one that replenishes and rejuvenates you from the inside out. Let this week be a reminder of the importance of water in your daily life and the positive effects it has on your overall health and happiness.

WEEK 25: VOLUNTEERING AND GIVING BACK

date:

Cultivating Compassion and Connection through Giving

Welcome to Week 25, where we focus on the heartwarming act of volunteering and giving back. This week is about extending our care and compassion beyond ourselves and touching the lives of others. Volunteering is not just an act of kindness towards others; it's a profound way to enrich our own lives. <u>Studies have shown that engaging in altruistic activities like volunteering can significantly boost our mental and emotional well-being, enhancing feelings of happiness, purpose, and connectedness.</u> This week, we invite you to explore the joy and fulfillment that comes from making a positive impact in your community and the world.

Nurturing the Spirit of Generosity and Service

1. <u>Finding a Cause:</u> Identify a cause or organization that resonates with your values and interests. This could be related to the environment, animal welfare, social justice, or community support.
2. <u>Committing Time:</u> Decide how much time you can realistically commit to volunteering. Even a few hours a month can make a significant difference.
3. <u>Skill-Based Volunteering:</u> Consider using your unique skills and talents to contribute. This could be anything from teaching, crafting, gardening, or administrative work.
4. <u>Acts of Kindness:</u> Remember that volunteering doesn't always require formal arrangements. Simple acts of kindness in your daily life are also valuable.

Exploring the Impact of Altruism on Self and Others

How do I feel when I am able to help others?
Reflect on the emotions and sense of fulfillment you experience when giving back.

Think about ways to incorporate small acts of kindness and generosity into your daily routine.

Weekly Goal

Your goal this week is to engage in at least one act of volunteering or giving back. Let this experience be an opportunity to connect with others, contribute to the greater good, and nurture your own well-being through the act of service.

As you embark on this journey of volunteering and giving, remember that every act of kindness, no matter how small, has the power to make a significant impact. Embrace this week as a chance to step outside of yourself, to connect, to give, and to grow. In giving, we often receive much more than we offer – a sense of purpose, connection, and the deep joy that comes from being part of something larger than ourselves.

WEEK 26: MID-YEAR REFLECTION

date:

Embracing the Journey: Reflecting on the First Half of the Year

Welcome to Week 26, a special time for mid-year reflection. As we reach the halfway point of our 52-week journey, it's a perfect moment to pause, look back, and appreciate the path we've traveled so far. Reflecting on our experiences and growth is a vital part of self-care. It helps us recognize our achievements, learn from our challenges, and realign with our goals and aspirations. <u>Research has shown that regular reflection enhances self-awareness, fosters learning, and can increase happiness and satisfaction in life.</u> This week, we lovingly turn inward to honor our journey and prepare for the journey ahead.

Nurturing Growth Through Thoughtful Reflection

1. <u>Reviewing Past Weeks:</u> Revisit the self-care activities and themes from the past 25 weeks. Reflect on which practices resonated with you the most and why.
2. <u>Journaling Your Journey:</u> Write in your journal about your experiences, changes, and insights since the beginning of the year. Celebrate your growth and acknowledge the challenges.
3. <u>Gratitude Practice:</u> Identify and write down the aspects of the first half of the year for which you are grateful. Gratitude can shift your perspective and open your heart to positivity.
4. <u>Setting Intentions for the Remaining Year:</u> Based on your reflections, set intentions or adjust your goals for the next half of the year. What would you like to focus on or explore further?

Deepening Your Understanding of Your Personal Journey

How have I grown or changed since the beginning of the year?
Reflect on personal developments, changes in perspectives, or new habits formed.

How can I apply these reflections to enhance my well-being for the rest of the year?

Weekly Goal

Your goal for this week is to take time for deep reflection on your journey so far and set thoughtful intentions for the coming months. Let this reflection be a loving and compassionate review of your story, celebrating your resilience, growth, and the path you are creating.

As you engage in this mid-year reflection, approach it with kindness and an open heart. Remember that self-care is not about perfection, but about growth, learning, and self-compassion. Each step you've taken, each challenge you've faced, is a part of your beautiful and unique journey. Honor your progress, learn from your experiences, and look forward to the rest of the year with hope, enthusiasm, and a renewed sense of purpose.

WEEK 27: EXPLORING NEW CULTURES

date:

Embracing Diversity and Enrichment through Cultural Exploration

Welcome to Week 27, a week dedicated to the exploration and appreciation of different cultures. Delving into new cultures is a wonderful way to expand our horizons, gain new perspectives, and connect with the rich tapestry of humanity. Engaging with diverse cultures can enhance empathy, increase awareness, and contribute to a sense of global connectedness. <u>Research in psychology and sociology highlights that cultural exposure can reduce biases and stereotypes, promoting open-mindedness and understanding.</u> This week, we invite you to immerse yourself in the beauty and diversity of the world's cultures, celebrating our shared humanity and the unique differences that enrich our lives.

Nurturing Global Awareness and Connection

1. <u>Cultural Research:</u> Choose a culture different from your own and spend time researching its traditions, history, and customs. This can be through books, documentaries, or online resources.
2. <u>Cultural Cuisine:</u> Explore a cuisine you're unfamiliar with. Try cooking a traditional dish at home or visit a restaurant that offers authentic flavors from that culture.
3. <u>Music and Art:</u> Discover the music, art, and literature of the culture. Listen to traditional music, view artwork, or read literature that is significant to that cultural background.
4. <u>Community Engagement:</u> Attend a cultural festival or community event, if available. Engaging with people from different cultures directly can be a deeply enriching experience.

Deepening Cultural Understanding and Empathy

How does learning about different cultures enrich my understanding of the world? Reflect on the new perspectives and insights gained from exploring other cultures.

How can I incorporate a celebration of diversity into my daily life?

Weekly Goal

Your goal for this week is to actively engage in learning about a new culture. Let this exploration be a journey of curiosity, empathy, and respect. Embrace the diversity of the world as a source of learning, inspiration, and connection.

As you embark on this week of cultural exploration, approach each experience with an open heart and mind. Remember, every culture holds its own beauty, wisdom, and stories. By exploring and appreciating the richness of different cultures, we not only broaden our own perspectives but also foster a deeper sense of global unity and compassion. Let this week be a celebration of the diverse and vibrant tapestry of humanity.

WEEK 28: GARDENING AND PLANT CARE

Nurturing Growth and Well-being through the Magic of Gardening

Welcome to Week 28, where we connect with the earth and embrace the nurturing practice of gardening and plant care. Gardening is not just about cultivating plants; it's about cultivating patience, care, and a deeper connection with nature. This practice offers a unique blend of physical activity, relaxation, and satisfaction. Research has shown that gardening can significantly reduce stress, improve mood, and even enhance cognitive function. It's a grounding activity that connects us to the cycles of nature and the joy of nurturing life. This week, we invite you to experience the therapeutic benefits of tending to plants and watching them flourish.

Cultivating Serenity and Growth in Your Garden

1. Starting a Small Garden: Begin with a small gardening project. This could be a container garden, a few potted plants, or a small patch in your yard.
2. Mindful Gardening: Practice mindfulness as you garden. Notice the texture of the soil, the fragrance of the plants, and the sensations of your hands as you work.
3. Plant Care Routine: Create a routine for plant care. Regular watering, pruning, and tending to your plants can be a calming and fulfilling ritual.
4. Learning About Your Plants: Take time to learn about the specific needs of your plants. Understanding what each plant needs to thrive can deepen your connection with them.

Reflecting on the Lessons and Joys of Gardening

How does caring for plants affect my mood and stress levels?
Notice any feelings of calmness, accomplishment, or joy that arise from gardening.

Consider how the patience, care, and attention you give to your plants can be applied to your relationships, work, or self-care practices.

Weekly Goal

Your goal for this week is to spend time each day tending to your plants or garden. Let this activity be a source of relaxation, joy, and connection to the natural world. Embrace each moment of gardening as an opportunity to nurture and be nurtured by the life you help grow.

As you immerse yourself in the world of gardening this week, allow yourself to be present in the simplicity and beauty of the process. Gardening is a gentle reminder of the interconnectedness of all life and the wonder of nature's cycles. It's a practice that not only beautifies your surroundings but also enriches your soul. Let the act of gardening be a loving ritual, a time to slow down, breathe, and appreciate the small yet profound miracles of life.

WEEK 29: MINDFUL EATING

Savoring Each Bite: The Journey of Mindful Eating

Welcome to Week 29, where we embrace the practice of mindful eating. Mindful eating is about experiencing food more intensely and with full awareness. It involves paying attention to the sensory experiences associated with food, from its preparation to its consumption. This practice can transform our relationship with food from mere sustenance to a source of pleasure and nourishment. Scientific research has shown that mindful eating can help improve digestion, reduce overeating, enhance the enjoyment of food, and contribute to a healthier relationship with what we eat. This week, we invite you to slow down, savor each bite, and fully engage with the experience of eating.

Nourishing Body and Soul Through Mindful Eating

1. Eating Without Distractions: Choose at least one meal per day to eat without distractions like TV, phones, or computers. Focus solely on the experience of eating.
2. Engaging All Your Senses: Pay attention to the colors, textures, smells, and flavors of your food. Notice the sensations as you chew.
3. Eating Slowly: Take your time with each bite, chewing thoroughly and pausing between bites to appreciate the food.
4. Mindful Food Preparation: Be present during the preparation of your meals. Appreciate the ingredients and the process of cooking as part of the eating experience.

Deepening Your Connection with Food and Eating

How does mindful eating change my experience of meals?
Reflect on any differences in satisfaction, enjoyment, or digestion when eating mindfully.

How can mindful eating support my overall wellness goals?
Consider how this practice can contribute to your physical, emotional, and mental health.

Weekly Goal

Your goal for this week is to practice mindful eating with at least one meal each day. Approach this practice as a form of self-care, an opportunity to nourish your body and mind with attention and gratitude. Let the act of eating become a mindful journey of discovery and appreciation.

As you engage in mindful eating this week, allow yourself to fully experience the joy and nourishment that food provides. This practice is not only about eating but also about cultivating an attitude of mindfulness that can extend to other areas of life. Embrace each meal as an opportunity to connect with the present moment, to care for your body, and to celebrate the simple pleasures of life.

WEEK 30: EXPLORING PHOTOGRAPHY

date:

Capturing Moments and Expressing Creativity through Photography

Welcome to Week 30, a week dedicated to the art and joy of photography. Photography is a powerful medium for self-expression and capturing the beauty of the world around us. It allows us to see life through a different lens, literally and metaphorically. Engaging in photography can be a mindful practice, encouraging us to slow down, observe our surroundings, and connect with moments we might otherwise overlook. Studies have shown that creative activities like photography can enhance our mood, boost self-esteem, and provide a sense of accomplishment. This week, we invite you to explore the world with your camera, expressing your unique perspective and finding beauty in both the ordinary and extraordinary.

Nurturing Creativity and Mindfulness through the Lens

1. Daily Photo Walks: Take a daily walk with the intention of capturing photographs. This could be in your neighborhood, a local park, or any place that inspires you.
2. Focusing on Details: Pay attention to the small details around you – the texture of a leaf, the patterns of shadows, the expressions of people.
3. Experimenting with Perspectives: Try photographing subjects from different angles and distances. Discover how changing perspectives can alter the story a photo tells.
4. Reflecting on Your Photos: Spend time reviewing the photos you take. Notice what emotions, thoughts, or memories they evoke.

Exploring Your Photographic Journey

How does photography influence the way I see the world?
Reflect on whether photography helps you notice details or aspects of your environment you usually miss.

Consider how photography can be a meditative practice and a form of expressing your inner self.

Weekly Goal

Set a goal to engage in photography each day this week, whether it's taking a few thoughtful shots each day or dedicating time for a longer photo walk. Let this practice be an exploration of creativity and a celebration of the world as seen through your eyes.

As you embark on this week of photography, allow yourself to be fully present in the experience. Each photo you take is a reflection of your perspective, a moment of connection with your surroundings, and a celebration of the beauty that exists all around. Embrace photography not just as a hobby, but as a mindful journey of discovery and self-expression.

WEEK 31: DANCE AND MOVEMENT THERAPY

date:

Embracing Healing and Joy through Dance and Movement

Welcome to Week 31, where we celebrate the transformative power of dance and movement therapy. This week is about discovering the joy and therapeutic benefits of expressing ourselves through movement. <u>Dance is not just physical exercise; it's a powerful form of self-expression that can liberate emotions, reduce stress, and promote mental and emotional well-being.</u> Research in the field of psychotherapy has shown that dance and movement therapy can enhance body awareness, improve mood, and facilitate emotional release. This week, we encourage you to let your body move freely, to explore the rhythms and movements that resonate with your soul, and to embrace dance as a path to inner harmony and self-discovery.

Finding Freedom and Healing in Movement

1. <u>Exploring Different Forms of Dance:</u> Experiment with various types of dance - from freeform or interpretive dance to more structured styles like salsa, hip-hop, or ballet.
2. <u>Creating a Safe Space:</u> Find or create a comfortable space where you feel free to move without inhibition or judgment.
3. <u>Intuitive Movement Sessions:</u> Allow yourself to move spontaneously to music that resonates with you. Let your body lead the way, not worrying about technique or form.
4. <u>Reflective Movement:</u> After dancing, take time to sit quietly and reflect on your experience. Notice any emotions or thoughts that emerged during your dance.

Understanding the Impact of Dance on Your Well-being

How do I feel physically and emotionally after dancing?
Reflect on any changes in your energy levels, mood, or sense of well-being.

Consider how incorporating regular dance into your life can support your overall health and happiness.

Weekly Goal

Set a goal to engage in some form of dance and movement therapy each day this week. Whether it's a few minutes of freeform movement or a structured dance session, approach this practice as an opportunity for self-expression, healing, and joy.

As you explore dance and movement this week, remember that this practice is about connection – with your body, your emotions, and your inner self. Dance allows you to express what words cannot, to release stored emotions, and to celebrate your existence in its most primal form. Embrace each movement as a loving gesture towards yourself, a way to nurture your body and soul through the beautiful language of dance.

WEEK 32: SELF-DEFENSE AND EMPOWERMENT

date:

Fostering Strength and Confidence through Self-Defense

Welcome to Week 32, a week dedicated to the empowering practice of self-defense. Learning self-defense is not only about physical techniques; it's about cultivating a sense of personal strength, confidence, and empowerment. Engaging in self-defense training can significantly enhance your sense of safety and self-efficacy. <u>Research has shown that self-defense skills can lead to increased self-esteem, reduced fear of victimization, and a greater feeling of personal autonomy.</u> This week, we encourage you to explore self-defense as a form of self-care, embracing it as a tool for building confidence, resilience, and a deep sense of personal empowerment.

Building Confidence and Strength through Self-Defense

1. <u>Exploring Self-Defense Classes:</u> Look for local self-defense classes or online tutorials that cater to beginners. Many styles are available, from martial arts to more modern self-defense techniques.
2. <u>Learning Basic Techniques:</u> Start with foundational self-defense moves. Focus on learning a few techniques well, such as how to break free from a grip or how to block an attack.
3. <u>Practicing Regularly:</u> Dedicate time each week to practice these techniques. Consistency is key to building confidence and muscle memory.
4. <u>Mindset Training:</u> Along with physical techniques, work on developing a confident, assertive mindset. Self-defense is as much about mental strength as it is about physical ability.

Empowering Yourself Through Self-Defense

How do I feel about my ability to protect and assert myself?
Reflect on your current feelings about your personal safety and empowerment.

Consider how the assertiveness, awareness, and confidence gained from self-defense can be beneficial in other contexts.

Weekly Goal

<u>Your goal for this week is to begin learning and practicing self-defense techniques</u>. Approach this practice with an attitude of empowerment, recognizing that each step you take is a commitment to your personal safety and self-confidence.

As you engage in self-defense training this week, remember that you are nurturing not just physical strength but also inner resilience. <u>This journey is about more than learning how to protect yourself; it's about embracing your power, honoring your worth, and cultivating a deep sense of self-respect and confidence.</u> Let each practice be a celebration of your strength and a testament to your commitment to self-care and personal empowerment.

WEEK 33: LANGUAGE LEARNING

Expanding Horizons through the Joy of Language Learning

Welcome to Week 33, a week dedicated to the enriching and rewarding experience of language learning. <u>Diving into a new language is not just about acquiring communication skills; it's an adventure into a different world, offering insights into new cultures, ways of thinking, and perspectives.</u> The process of learning a new language has been shown to enhance cognitive abilities, improve memory, and even delay the onset of certain mental aging processes. Embracing language learning is a wonderful act of self-care, providing mental stimulation, a sense of achievement, and the potential for deeper connections with people across the globe. This week, we invite you to begin or continue your journey with a new language, exploring the beauty and intricacies it has to offer.

Cultivating Cognitive Growth and Cultural Understanding

1. <u>Choosing a Language:</u> Select a language that interests you, whether it's due to personal heritage, travel goals, or simply curiosity.
2. <u>Setting Realistic Goals:</u> Start with small, achievable goals. This could be learning basic greetings, numbers, or common phrases.
3. <u>Utilizing Resources:</u> Make use of the wide range of available resources, such as language learning apps, online courses, books, or language exchange meetups.
4. <u>Daily Practice:</u> Dedicate a regular time each day for language study, even if it's just a few minutes. Consistency is key in language learning.

Exploring the Impact of Language Learning on Self-Development

How does learning a new language challenge and stimulate me?
Reflect on the mental and emotional aspects of engaging with a new language.

Think about the ways in which knowing another language could open up new opportunities and connections.

Weekly Goal

Your goal for this week is to establish a regular routine for language study and immerse yourself in the learning process. Whether it's learning new words, phrases, or grammatical structures, view each step as an exciting progress in your journey of linguistic exploration.

As you embark on this language learning journey, remember to be patient and kind to yourself. Learning a new language is a journey of discovery, filled with both challenges and triumphs. Each word you learn, each sentence you construct, is a bridge to a wider world, a step towards greater understanding, and a celebration of your dedication to personal growth and cultural exploration.

WEEK 34: MINDFUL WALKING AND HIKING

date:

Embracing the Path of Mindfulness in Every Step

Welcome to Week 34, a week to connect with the simple yet profound practice of mindful walking and hiking. <u>This activity is not just about physical exercise; it's an opportunity to cultivate mindfulness, presence, and a deep connection with the environment.</u> Walking and hiking mindfully can offer significant benefits for mental and physical health, including reducing stress, enhancing mood, and improving overall well-being. This week, we encourage you to step outside, be it in nature or your local neighborhood, and transform your walks into meditative, rejuvenating journeys.

Nurturing Mind and Body Through Mindful Movement

1. <u>Choosing Your Environment:</u> Select a place for your mindful walk or hike, whether it's a quiet path, a park, or even a busy street. Each environment offers unique stimuli for mindfulness.
2. <u>Engaging Your Senses:</u> As you walk, fully immerse yourself in the experience. Notice the sights, sounds, smells, and the feel of the ground beneath your feet.
3. <u>Paced Breathing:</u> Sync your breathing with your steps. Inhale for a few steps and exhale for a few, creating a rhythmic pattern that anchors your mind in the present moment.
4. <u>Observing Thoughts and Sensations:</u> When you notice your mind wandering, gently bring your attention back to the act of walking and the sensations in your body.

Exploring the Inner Journey of Mindful Walking

How does mindful walking affect my mental and emotional state?
Reflect on any changes in your stress levels, mood, or thought patterns after a mindful walk.

How can I integrate mindful walking into my daily routine?

Weekly Goal

Your goal for this week is to engage in mindful walking or hiking regularly. Let each step be a gentle reminder to be present and connected, to the world around you and within you. Embrace this time as a precious opportunity for reflection, rejuvenation, and connection.

As you embark on your mindful walks this week, remember that each step is an opportunity to ground yourself in the present moment, to find peace in the rhythm of your movement, and to cherish the beauty of the world around you. Let these walks be a sanctuary for your mind, a space where you can release stress, connect with nature, and nurture a sense of inner calm and clarity.

WEEK 35: DEEP CLEANING AND DECLUTTERING

Creating Clarity and Harmony in Your Personal Space

Welcome to Week 35, a week dedicated to the nurturing practices of deep cleaning and decluttering. This week is about more than just tidying up; it's a process of creating an environment that reflects and supports your inner peace. The act of cleaning and organizing our personal spaces can be incredibly therapeutic. Research has shown that a clutter-free and clean environment can significantly impact our mental well-being, reducing stress and anxiety, and promoting a sense of control and calm. Let's embrace the transformative power of decluttering and cleaning, viewing it as a physical manifestation of self-care and an expression of respect for our living spaces.

Fostering a Refreshed and Organized Environment

1. Identifying Areas for Decluttering: Choose specific areas in your home or workspace that need attention. This could be a closet, a desk, or an entire room.
2. Mindful Decluttering: As you sort through items, ask yourself whether each item is useful, brings joy, or is no longer needed. Donate, recycle, or discard items accordingly.
3. Deep Cleaning: After decluttering, give these spaces a thorough cleaning. Notice how cleaning can be a meditative and satisfying activity.
4. Organizing with Intention: Organize the remaining items thoughtfully. Consider how the organization can contribute to a more peaceful and functional space.

Contemplating the Impact of Your Environment on Well-being

How does the state of my environment affect my mood and productivity?
Reflect on how clutter and cleanliness influence your mental state and daily activities.

How can maintaining an organized space support my overall wellness?

Weekly Goal

Set a goal to declutter and clean a specific area of your space this week. Approach this task not as a chore but as an act of self-love and a commitment to creating a harmonious environment. Recognize the value of this process in fostering a sense of calm and order in your life.

As you engage in deep cleaning and decluttering this week, remember that each action is a step towards creating a sanctuary for yourself. A clean and organized space can be a source of tranquility and a reflection of your inner state. Embrace this opportunity to clear out the old and make space for new energy and possibilities in your life. Let the process be a therapeutic journey, one that nurtures both your environment and your soul.

WEEK 36: POSITIVE VISUALIZATION

Cultivating a Future of Hope and Happiness through Visualization

Welcome to Week 36, a week where we embrace the transformative practice of positive visualization. Visualization is a powerful tool for personal growth and manifesting positive changes in our lives. It involves creating vivid and positive mental images of the outcomes we desire, which can help align our thoughts and actions towards achieving these goals. Scientific research has shown that regular positive visualization can enhance motivation, increase confidence, and improve performance. It's a practice that not only shapes our future aspirations but also enriches our present moments with hope and positivity. This week, let's embark on a journey of visualization, fostering a mindset of optimism and possibility.

Embracing Your Dreams through Visualization

1. Creating a Visualization Routine: Dedicate a few minutes each day to practice positive visualization. Find a quiet, comfortable space where you can relax and focus.
2. Crafting Your Vision: Visualize scenarios where you have achieved your goals. Imagine the details – the setting, the emotions, the sensations.
3. Incorporating All Senses: Make your visualization as vivid as possible by involving all your senses. What do you see, hear, feel, and perhaps even taste or smell?
4. Affirmations and Visualization: Combine visualization with positive affirmations. Reinforce your visualized goals with affirming statements about your ability to achieve them.

Exploring the Power of Your Imagination

How do I feel after practicing positive visualization?
Reflect on any changes in your mood, confidence, or outlook on life.

Consider practical steps you can take to bring your visualizations closer to reality.

Weekly Goal

Your goal for this week is to engage in positive visualization every day. Let this practice be a source of inspiration and a reminder of your potential and power to shape your future. Embrace each session as an opportunity to plant seeds of positivity and growth in your life.

As you engage in positive visualization this week, remember that your thoughts and visions are powerful catalysts for change. Each visualization is a step towards manifesting the life you desire and deserve. Allow yourself to dream big, to believe in your visions, and to feel the joy and fulfillment of your imagined successes. This practice is not just about the future; it's a celebration of your ability to create and shape your reality with hope and intention.

WEEK 37: EXPLORING LOCAL ATTRACTIONS

date:

Rediscovering Joy and Wonder in Your Local Surroundings

Welcome to Week 37, a week dedicated to the delightful exploration of local attractions. Often, the most beautiful and interesting places are right in our own backyards, waiting to be discovered or revisited with fresh eyes. Exploring local attractions is not just about sightseeing; it's an opportunity to reconnect with your community, appreciate your environment, and find joy in the familiar and the overlooked. Research has shown that engaging with one's local culture and environment can boost happiness, enhance a sense of belonging, and provide a refreshing break from the daily routine. This week, let's embark on a journey of local exploration, celebrating the unique beauty and experiences our immediate surroundings have to offer.

Nurturing Curiosity and Connection in Your Community

1. Researching Local Points of Interest: Look up local attractions, historical sites, parks, or unique landmarks. Plan a visit to places you haven't explored yet or would like to see again.
2. Taking a Walking Tour: Consider taking a walking tour of your town or city, whether guided or self-directed. Pay attention to the architecture, street art, and hidden gems.
3. Visiting Local Museums or Galleries: Spend an afternoon at a local museum or art gallery, immersing yourself in the culture and history of your area.
4. Enjoying Nature Locally: If nature attractions are accessible, plan a visit. This could be a local nature reserve, a botanical garden, or a scenic hiking trail.

Contemplating the Richness of Your Local Environment

What new things did I discover about my local area?
Reflect on any new insights, histories, or perspectives you gained about your surroundings.

Think about ways to continue discovering and enjoying local attractions in your routine.

Weekly Goal

Your goal for this week is to visit and appreciate at least one local attraction. Approach these explorations with a sense of wonder and openness, allowing yourself to be intrigued and inspired by the richness of your immediate world.

As you explore your local attractions this week, embrace each experience as an opportunity to deepen your connection with your community and its history. Allow yourself to marvel at the beauty and diversity that lies just a step away from your daily path. This journey of local exploration is a celebration of the familiar, a rediscovery of the treasures that surround you, and a loving homage to the place you call home.

WEEK 38: BAKING AND CULINARY ARTS

date:

Nourishing the Soul Through the Art of Baking and Cooking

Welcome to Week 38, where we immerse ourselves in the creative and nurturing world of baking and the culinary arts. This week is about more than just preparing food; it's an opportunity to express creativity, experience sensory pleasure, and provide nourishment in a deeply personal way. <u>Engaging in baking and cooking can be a therapeutic and meditative experience.</u> Research has shown that culinary activities can help reduce stress, boost mood, and enhance mindfulness. The act of creating a dish, from the careful measuring of ingredients to the joy of sharing the final product, can be a fulfilling journey of discovery and satisfaction. Let's embrace the kitchen as a place of creativity, comfort, and connection.

Exploring Creativity and Comfort in the Kitchen

1. <u>Trying New Recipes:</u> Choose a new recipe that intrigues you, whether it's a type of bread, a complex dish, or a simple, comforting meal.
2. <u>Mindful Cooking:</u> As you cook or bake, focus fully on the process. Notice the textures, aromas, and sounds, and enjoy the rhythm of the culinary activity.
3. <u>Artistic Plating:</u> Experiment with plating your dishes in an artistic way. This not only enhances the visual appeal but also celebrates the effort you've put into the cooking.
4. <u>Sharing Your Creations:</u> If possible, share your culinary creations with friends or family. Cooking for others can be an act of love and a way to strengthen connections.

Savoring the Experience of Culinary Arts

How does cooking or baking affect my emotional well-being?

Think about ways to make culinary activities a more frequent and cherished part of your life.

Weekly Goal

Set a goal this week to engage in a baking or cooking project. Let this activity be a canvas for your creativity and a source of comfort and joy. Embrace the process as a nurturing act for both body and soul.

As you delve into the world of baking and cooking this week, let each ingredient, each step, be a mindful practice of care and creativity. Allow yourself to experiment, to savor the flavors and aromas, and to find joy in the creation of something beautiful and delicious. Remember, every dish you prepare is a reflection of your creativity and an expression of self-care, nourishing not just your body but also your spirit.

WEEK 39: BOARD GAMES AND PUZZLES

Engaging the Mind and Spirit with Games and Puzzles

Welcome to Week 39, a week dedicated to the joy and mental stimulation of board games and puzzles. These activities are not just entertaining pastimes; they offer a unique blend of cognitive challenge and playful exploration. <u>Engaging in games and puzzles has been shown to improve memory, problem-solving skills, and even emotional well-being.</u> They provide an opportunity for mindful focus, creative thinking, and, when shared with others, a chance for laughter and connection. This week, we invite you to embrace the fun and benefits of board games and puzzles, seeing them as tools for relaxation, mental engagement, and strengthening bonds with friends and family.

Exploring Fun and Connection Through Play

1. <u>Choosing Games or Puzzles:</u> Select a board game or puzzle that interests you. It could be a strategy game, a classic puzzle, or something new and intriguing.
2. <u>Solo Puzzling:</u> If you're engaging in puzzles alone, find a quiet time to focus on the challenge. Notice the satisfaction of finding the right piece or solving a problem.
3. <u>Game Nights with Loved Ones:</u> Organize a game night with friends or family. This is a great way to connect, laugh, and create memories.
4. <u>Mindful Gaming:</u> Whether playing alone or with others, be fully present during the game. Pay attention to the game's details and enjoy the process, regardless of winning or losing.

Discovering the Benefits of Games and Puzzles in Your Life

How do I feel during and after engaging in games or puzzles?
Reflect on any changes in your mood, stress levels, or sense of accomplishment.

Consider how games and puzzles can be used for quality family time, relaxation, or personal growth.

Weekly Goal

Your goal for this week is to spend some time playing board games or solving puzzles. Let these activities be a joyful break from the routine, a way to engage your mind, and an opportunity for meaningful interaction with others.

As you immerse yourself in the world of games and puzzles this week, remember that the true value lies in the journey, not just the outcome. Each move in a game, each piece of a puzzle, is a step in a delightful dance of thought and strategy. Embrace these moments of play and mental challenge as nurturing experiences, enriching your mind and fostering connections with those around you. Let laughter, strategy, and the joy of solving be your companions in this week of playful exploration.

WEEK 40: ACTS OF KINDNESS

Spreading Light with Simple Acts of Kindness

Welcome to Week 40, a special week dedicated to the heartfelt practice of performing acts of kindness. Engaging in acts of kindness isn't just beneficial for those on the receiving end; it's a deeply fulfilling and enriching experience for the giver too. Scientific studies have shown that performing acts of kindness can boost happiness, reduce stress, and even improve physical health. This week, we encourage you to look for opportunities to spread kindness in big or small ways. Each act of kindness is like a ripple in a pond, with the potential to spread far and wide, creating a more compassionate and loving world.

Fostering Compassion and Connection Through Kindness

1. Random Acts of Kindness: Each day, find a way to perform a random act of kindness. This could be as simple as a warm smile to a stranger, offering a compliment, or helping someone in need.
2. Kindness in Communication: Be mindful of your words. Offer encouragement, express gratitude, or send a thoughtful message to someone.
3. Volunteering Time or Resources: If possible, volunteer your time or resources to a cause or individual who could benefit from your support.
4. Self-Kindness: Remember to include yourself in your acts of kindness. Practice self-compassion and recognize your own worth and needs.

Exploring the Impact of Kindness in Your Life

How do I feel when I engage in acts of kindness?
Reflect on the emotional and psychological effects of being kind to others and yourself.

Think about how you can integrate kindness into your daily routine in sustainable and meaningful ways.

Weekly Goal

Set a goal to practice acts of kindness throughout the week. Approach each act with a loving heart, viewing it as an opportunity to make a positive impact on others and yourself. Let this week be a reminder of the power of kindness to transform lives, including your own.

As you engage in acts of kindness this week, let each gesture be a beacon of love and compassion. Remember, every act of kindness, no matter how small, contributes to a warmer, more compassionate world. Embrace this practice not just as a way to help others, but as a profound method of self-care, nurturing your spirit and deepening your connection with the world around you. Let the joy of giving and receiving kindness be a guiding light in your journey.

WEEK 41: BIRD WATCHING AND WILDLIFE OBSERVATION

Discovering Serenity and Wonder in Nature's Symphony

Welcome to Week 41, where we immerse ourselves in the peaceful and rewarding activity of bird watching and wildlife observation. This week is about connecting with the natural world, appreciating the beauty of wildlife, and finding tranquility in the simplicity of nature. Engaging with nature through bird watching and observing wildlife can be a meditative and joyous experience. Research has shown that spending time in nature, observing wildlife, can reduce stress, improve mood, and enhance our overall sense of well-being. It's a chance to slow down, be present, and marvel at the wonders of the natural world.

Nurturing a Connection with Nature Through Observation

1. Finding a Spot for Observation: Choose a location that is known for its wildlife, such as a local park, nature reserve, or even your own backyard.
2. Equipping Yourself: If possible, use binoculars or a camera to enhance your wildlife watching experience. A field guide can also be helpful in identifying different species.
3. Practicing Patience and Stillness: Spend time quietly observing. Patience is key in wildlife observation – the longer you wait, the more you are likely to see.
4. Recording Your Observations: Consider keeping a nature journal to note your observations, thoughts, and feelings during these excursions.

Exploring the Impact of Nature Observation on Your Spirit

How does spending time observing nature affect my emotional state?
Reflect on any changes in your stress levels, sense of peace, or joy.

How can I incorporate nature observation into my regular self-care routine?
Think about ways to make wildlife watching a more frequent and integral part of your life.

Weekly Goal

Your goal for this week is to dedicate time to bird watching and wildlife observation. Let these moments be an opportunity to connect with nature, to experience the world beyond human concerns, and to find a sense of peace and wonder.

As you engage in bird watching and wildlife observation this week, allow yourself to be fully present in the experience. Let the sights and sounds of nature envelop you, providing a sanctuary of peace and beauty. Each observation is an invitation to slow down, breathe, and appreciate the simple yet profound wonders of the natural world. Embrace this practice as a loving journey into the heart of nature, where every bird's song and every rustle in the underbrush is a reminder of the intricate and beautiful tapestry of life.

WEEK 42: CALLIGRAPHY AND HAND LETTERING

date:

Embracing the Artistic Flow of Calligraphy and Hand Lettering

Welcome to Week 42, a week to delve into the graceful and meditative art of calligraphy and hand lettering. This practice is more than just writing; it's a form of artistic expression that combines creativity with mindfulness. Engaging in calligraphy and hand lettering can be a soothing and fulfilling activity, offering a space for concentration and artistic exploration. Studies have shown that engaging in creative arts like calligraphy can reduce stress, improve mental clarity, and enhance emotional well-being. This week, let's explore the elegant dance of pen and ink, allowing ourselves to get lost in the beauty of creating each letter and word.

Cultivating Creativity and Mindfulness through Writing

1. Gathering Supplies: Start with basic supplies like a calligraphy pen, ink, and smooth paper. For hand lettering, markers or pens of various sizes can be useful.
2. Learning the Basics: Begin with simple strokes and practice making basic letter forms. Online tutorials or calligraphy books can be excellent guides.
3. Mindful Practice: As you write, focus on the flow of the pen and the formation of each letter. Let this practice be a mindful activity where you are fully present in the moment.
4. Creating a Project: Work on a small project, like a hand-lettered quote or a written letter to a friend. Let this project be an expression of your new skill and creativity.

Discovering the Joys of Calligraphy and Hand Lettering

How does the practice of calligraphy or hand lettering make me feel?
Reflect on any feelings of relaxation, satisfaction, or joy that arise during your practice.

How can I incorporate this art form into my regular self-care routine?
Think about ways to make calligraphy or hand lettering a regular part of your life, whether it's through journaling, creating art, or writing letters.

Weekly Goal

Your goal for this week is to dedicate time to practicing calligraphy or hand lettering. Let this practice be a journey of artistic expression, a space for you to unwind and engage with the meditative flow of writing.

As you immerse yourself in calligraphy and hand lettering this week, embrace the process with patience and gentleness. Each stroke, each letter is a reflection of your presence and creativity. Allow yourself to find joy in the learning process, celebrating the unique beauty of your handcrafted letters and words. This artistic journey is not just about the final product; it's about finding peace and joy in the act of creation itself.

WEEK 43: MARTIAL ARTS OR TAI CHI

date:

Embracing Balance and Strength through Martial Arts and Tai Chi

Welcome to Week 43, a week to explore the disciplines of martial arts and Tai Chi. These practices are more than physical exercises; they are holistic approaches to well-being, blending physical movement, mental focus, and emotional balance. Engaging in martial arts or Tai Chi can provide a range of benefits, including improved physical fitness, stress reduction, and enhanced mental clarity. Research has shown that these disciplines can also promote self-discipline, boost self-esteem, and increase mindfulness. This week, let's step into the world of martial arts or Tai Chi, embracing the journey of personal growth and inner harmony they offer.

Cultivating Discipline, Focus, and Peace through Movement

1. Choosing a Practice: Decide whether you would like to explore a martial art or Tai Chi. Each offers a unique experience - martial arts being more dynamic and Tai Chi being more meditative.
2. Finding a Class or Resource: Look for a local class or online tutorial that caters to beginners. Many communities offer introductory courses in various martial arts and Tai Chi.
3. Regular Practice: Dedicate time each week to practice. Consistency is important in building skill and reaping the mental and physical benefits.
4. Mindful Movement: As you practice, focus on the movement and your breath. Be present in each posture and sequence, observing how your body feels.

Exploring the Impact of Martial Arts or Tai Chi on Your Well-being

How does practicing martial arts or Tai Chi affect my physical and mental state?
Reflect on changes in your energy levels, mood, and mental clarity.

Consider how the discipline, mindfulness, and balance can be integrated into your daily routine and interactions.

Weekly Goal

Your goal for this week is to engage in the practice of martial arts or Tai Chi, exploring how these disciplines enhance your physical, mental, and emotional well-being. Allow each session to be a step towards greater self-awareness, strength, and inner peace.

As you delve into martial arts or Tai Chi this week, approach each movement and posture as an opportunity to connect deeply with yourself. Let this practice be a harmonious blend of strength and serenity, a space where you can explore your limits and potentials. Remember, the journey in these disciplines is not just about physical prowess; it's about cultivating a balanced and centered spirit, ready to face life's challenges with grace and resilience.

WEEK 44: INDOOR PLANT CARE

Nurturing Well-being through the Care of Indoor Plants

Welcome to Week 44, where we turn our focus to the tender care of indoor plants. Tending to plants is a deeply rewarding and grounding activity, offering more than just aesthetic beauty to our living spaces. <ins>The presence of plants can have a calming effect, improving air quality and enhancing our connection with nature.</ins> Scientific studies have found that caring for plants can reduce stress, boost mood, and even improve concentration and productivity. This week, let's embrace the gentle art of indoor plant care, seeing it as a soothing and nurturing practice for both the plants and ourselves.

Cultivating a Green Sanctuary in Your Home

1. Selecting Plants: If you don't already have indoor plants, consider selecting a few that are known for their air-purifying qualities and suitability for indoor environments, such as snake plants or peace lilies.
2. Learning About Your Plants: Research the specific needs of each plant – their preferred light, water, and temperature conditions.
3. Regular Care Routine: Establish a routine for watering, pruning, and checking the health of your plants. Engaging regularly with your plants can be a meditative and rewarding practice.
4. Mindful Observation: Spend time observing your plants, noticing their growth, the texture of their leaves, and their overall health. This can be a practice in mindfulness and presence.

Exploring the Connection Between Plant Care and Self-Care

How does taking care of plants affect my emotional well-being?
Reflect on any feelings of calm, accomplishment, or joy that arise from caring for your plants.

Think about how the nurturing, attention to detail, and routine required for plant care can apply to your self-care practices.

Weekly Goal

Set a goal to spend time each day with your indoor plants. Whether it's watering, pruning, or simply enjoying their presence, let this time be an act of care for both your plants and yourself. Embrace the quiet satisfaction and sense of connection that comes from nurturing another living thing.

As you care for your plants this week, allow yourself to connect with the simple yet profound act of nurturing. Each moment spent with your plants is an opportunity to slow down, to breathe, and to appreciate the beauty and tranquility they bring into your space. Let the act of caring for your plants be a loving reminder of the importance of nurturing and growth, both in your plants and in yourself.

WEEK 45: EXPLORING PODCASTS AND AUDIOBOOKS

date:

Enriching the Mind and Soul through the World of Audio

Welcome to Week 45, where we dive into the enriching and diverse world of podcasts and audiobooks. This week is an invitation to explore new ideas, stories, and perspectives through the simple yet powerful medium of audio. Listening to podcasts and audiobooks can be a wonderful way to relax, learn, and entertain oneself. Research has shown that engaging with spoken word content can improve listening skills, increase empathy, and even enhance knowledge on various subjects. Whether it's for inspiration, education, or entertainment, podcasts and audiobooks offer a convenient way to enrich your daily life.

Nurturing Curiosity and Connection through Listening

1. Selecting Content: Choose podcasts or audiobooks that interest you. This could be in genres you enjoy or topics you're curious about, such as personal growth, history, science, or storytelling.
2. Creating a Listening Routine: Find a comfortable time and place for listening, such as during your commute, on a walk, or as part of your evening relaxation routine.
3. Reflective Listening: As you listen, reflect on the ideas or stories being presented. How do they resonate with your experiences or challenge your perspectives?
4. Discussion and Sharing: If possible, discuss interesting podcasts or audiobooks with friends or family. Sharing and discussing can deepen the experience.

Contemplating the Insights and Enjoyment from Audio Learning

How do podcasts or audiobooks influence my mood and thoughts?
Reflect on any changes in your emotional state or new ideas sparked by what you've listened to.

Think about ways to make podcasts and audiobooks a regular part of your personal growth and leisure time.

Weekly Goal

Your goal for this week is to incorporate podcasts or audiobooks into your daily routine. Let each listening session be an opportunity to learn something new, escape into a story, or gain different perspectives on life.

As you explore the world of podcasts and audiobooks this week, let each audio journey be a path to greater understanding, relaxation, and connection with the broader human experience. Embrace the simplicity and richness of listening, and allow the power of spoken words to inspire, educate, and entertain you. Each story, each piece of knowledge, is a gift that enriches your world from the inside out.

WEEK 46: CRAFTING AND DIY PROJECTS

date:

Embracing Creativity and Personal Expression through Crafting and DIY

Welcome to Week 46, a week dedicated to the joy and fulfillment found in crafting and DIY projects. Engaging in creative activities like crafting is not just a hobby; it's a form of self-expression and a way to engage our minds and hands in harmonious activity. The act of creating something, whether it's through knitting, woodworking, painting, or any other form of craft, can be incredibly therapeutic. Studies have shown that crafting can reduce stress, improve mood, and enhance cognitive function. It's a way of stepping back from the busyness of life and focusing on the present moment, immersing yourself in the process of creation.

Nurturing the Spirit through Creative Endeavors

1. Choosing a Project: Select a crafting or DIY project that excites you. It could be something as simple as a scrapbook, a piece of home decor, or a handmade gift.
2. Gathering Materials: Enjoy the process of gathering the materials you need. Each item is a building block in your creation.
3. Dedicated Crafting Time: Set aside dedicated time for your project. This is your time to unwind and engage in something purely for the joy of it.
4. Sharing Your Work: Consider sharing your finished project with others, whether it's displaying it in your home or giving it as a gift. Celebrate your accomplishment.

Exploring the Impact of Crafting on Your Well-being

How does engaging in crafting or DIY projects make me feel?
Reflect on any feelings of relaxation, satisfaction, or pride in your work.

Consider ways to incorporate crafting into your regular routine for continuous mental and emotional enrichment.

Weekly Goal

Your goal for this week is to start and engage with a crafting or DIY project. Let this activity be an avenue for self-expression, mindfulness, and a celebration of your unique creativity.

As you immerse yourself in your crafting project this week, embrace each moment as an opportunity to express yourself and create something meaningful. Remember, crafting is not just about the end product; it's about the process, the learning, and the joy found in creating. Allow yourself to explore, experiment, and take pride in your ability to bring something new into existence with your own hands and imagination.

WEEK 47: TEA TASTING AND APPRECIATION

date:

Savoring Moments of Peace and Pleasure with Tea

Welcome to Week 47, where we embrace the serene and delightful world of tea tasting and appreciation. Tea, with its vast array of flavors and aromas, offers more than just a beverage; it provides an experience, a ritual, and a moment of tranquility. The act of brewing and savoring tea can be a meditative practice, allowing us to slow down, relax, and engage our senses fully. Scientific studies have highlighted the health benefits of various teas, including stress reduction, antioxidant properties, and improved heart health. This week, let's journey through the world of tea, exploring its rich flavors and the peacefulness it brings to our daily lives.

Cultivating Mindfulness and Enjoyment in Tea Tasting

1. Exploring Different Teas: Choose a selection of different types of tea to try – this could include green, black, herbal, oolong, or white teas. Notice the different flavors, aromas, and colors.
2. Mindful Brewing: Pay attention to the process of brewing tea. Observe the color change in the water, the aroma that fills the air, and the warmth of the cup in your hands.
3. Savoring Each Sip: Drink your tea slowly, savoring each sip. Notice the taste and texture of the tea in your mouth and the sensation as you swallow.
4. Learning About Tea: Educate yourself about the origins, types, and traditions of tea. Understanding the history and culture behind tea can deepen your appreciation.

Discovering the Richness of Tea in Your Life

How does the ritual of tea tasting affect my mood and state of mind?

How can I incorporate the practice of tea tasting into my daily routine?

Weekly Goal

Set a goal to enjoy the practice of tea tasting daily this week. Let this time be a peaceful retreat from the hustle of everyday life, a moment to relax, rejuvenate, and indulge in the sensory pleasures of tea.

As you engage in the art of tea tasting this week, let each cup be a journey into mindfulness and serenity. Allow the ritual of brewing and tasting tea to be a moment of pause in your day, a space to breathe, reflect, and connect with yourself. Embrace the diversity and richness of tea, and let it be a source of calm, comfort, and pleasure in your daily routine.

WEEK 48: ASTRONOMY AND STARGAZING

date:

Gazing into the Cosmos: Finding Peace in the Stars

Welcome to Week 48, a week dedicated to the awe-inspiring practice of astronomy and stargazing. The act of looking up at the night sky offers more than just a visual spectacle; it's an opportunity to connect with the universe and contemplate our place in it. Stargazing can be a profoundly meditative and calming experience, allowing us to step away from the immediacy of daily life and marvel at the vastness of the cosmos. Research has shown that connecting with nature, including the celestial world, can reduce stress, enhance feelings of awe and wonder, and improve mental well-being. This week, let's turn our eyes skyward and find tranquility and perspective in the beauty of the night sky.

Exploring the Universe and Our Connection to It

1. Finding the Right Time and Place: Choose a clear night and a location away from city lights to optimize your stargazing experience.
2. Learning Basic Astronomy: Familiarize yourself with basic constellations, planets, and celestial events. Apps and guides can help you navigate the night sky.
3. Mindful Observation: Spend time quietly observing the stars. Notice their brightness, patterns, and the feelings they evoke in you.
4. Reflecting on the Universe: Use this time to reflect on the vastness of the universe and your connection to it. Contemplate the beauty and mystery of the cosmos.

Discovering the Depth and Wonder of the Night Sky

How does stargazing affect my sense of self and my perspective on life?
Reflect on any feelings of awe, humility, or a deeper sense of connection to the universe.

How can I incorporate the peace and perspective gained from stargazing into my daily life?
Consider ways to carry the tranquility and broader perspective into your everyday routine.

Weekly Goal

Your goal for this week is to spend time stargazing and contemplating the celestial wonders. Let this practice be a moment of peace and awe, a chance to connect with the universe and find tranquility in its vast beauty.
As you look up at the night sky this week, let the stars remind you of the endless mysteries and beauties of the universe. Embrace the sense of wonder and calm that comes from this connection, allowing it to fill you with a sense of peace and perspective. Remember, in the grand scale of the cosmos, our troubles can seem smaller, and our connection to something larger than ourselves can provide comfort and a sense of belonging in the vast tapestry of existence.

WEEK 49: TIME MANAGEMENT SKILLS

date:

Embracing the Gift of Time: Cultivating Effective Time Management

Welcome to Week 49, a week dedicated to developing and enhancing time management skills. Time is one of our most precious resources, and learning to use it effectively can greatly improve our quality of life. Good time management isn't just about being productive; it's about creating balance, reducing stress, and making space for the things that truly matter. Research has shown that effective time management leads to better work-life balance, lower levels of stress, and increased satisfaction with life. This week, let's focus on understanding and improving how we manage our time, so we can live more fully and mindfully.

Mastering the Art of Time Management for Well-being

1. Time Audit: Begin by tracking how you spend your time for a few days. This can help you identify areas where you might be losing time to unproductive activities.
2. Setting Priorities: Determine what tasks and activities are most important to you. Focus on aligning your time with these priorities.
3. Creating a Balanced Schedule: Make a schedule that includes time for work, leisure, self-care, and social activities. Remember, balance is key.
4. Learning to Say No: Practice saying no to tasks or activities that don't align with your priorities or that overextend your time.

Exploring the Impact of Time Management on Your Life

How do I feel when my time is well-managed versus when it is not?
Reflect on the emotional and physical differences you experience during times of effective versus poor time management.

How can improved time management enhance my daily life and overall well-being?

Weekly Goal

Set a goal this week to implement one or two new time management strategies. Focus on making small, sustainable changes that can lead to a more balanced and fulfilling use of your time.

As you work on improving your time management this week, approach this task with kindness and patience. Remember, the goal is not to fill every moment with productivity but to find a harmonious balance that supports your well-being and personal values. Embrace each day as an opportunity to live intentionally, making space for both your responsibilities and your joys.

WEEK 50: COLD WEATHER ACTIVITIES

Embracing the Beauty and Tranquility of the Cold Season

Welcome to Week 50, a time to find joy and comfort in cold weather activities. As the temperature drops, it can be tempting to retreat indoors, but the colder months offer unique opportunities for activities that can bring joy, invigoration, and a sense of wonder. Engaging in outdoor activities during the cold season can have numerous benefits, including improved mood, increased physical fitness, and an enhanced appreciation for the natural world. Whether it's a brisk walk in a winter wonderland or cozy indoor activities, this week is about embracing the unique beauty and opportunities that cold weather brings.

Nurturing Well-being with Seasonal Activities

1. Outdoor Exploration: Dress warmly and take a walk in a local park or nature trail. Notice the beauty of the natural landscape in its winter state.
2. Winter Sports: If accessible, try engaging in a winter sport like skiing, snowboarding, or ice skating. These activities can be exhilarating and offer a great way to stay active.
3. Indoor Coziness: Create a cozy indoor environment. Light candles, make hot cocoa, and spend time reading, crafting, or doing other relaxing activities.
4. Seasonal Photography: Capture the beauty of the cold season through photography. The winter landscape, with its unique light and shadows, can offer stunning photographic opportunities.

Contemplating the Season's Influence on Well-being

How do cold weather activities affect my mood and energy levels?
Reflect on any changes in your well-being after engaging in outdoor or cozy indoor activities.

How can I adapt my self-care routine to embrace the cold season?

Weekly Goal

Set a goal this week to actively participate in cold weather activities, whether outdoors or indoors. Let these activities be a way to celebrate the season, finding beauty and peace in the chilly weather and the unique experiences it offers.

As you engage in the activities of the cold season this week, embrace each moment with openness and appreciation. Let the crisp air, the quiet of a snow-covered landscape, or the warmth of a cozy room be reminders of the ever-changing beauty of nature and the opportunity to find joy in all seasons. Remember, each season brings its own gifts, and the cold months are no exception. Embrace this time as a special opportunity to nurture your body, mind, and soul in unique and fulfilling ways.

WEEK 51: REFLECTING ON PERSONAL GROWTH

date:

Celebrating Your Journey and Acknowledging Your Growth

Welcome to Week 51, a time for reflection and acknowledgment of the personal growth you've experienced throughout the year. As we approach the end of our 52-week self-care journey, it's important to look back and recognize the changes, challenges, and achievements we've encountered. Reflecting on personal growth helps us appreciate our resilience, learn from our experiences, and set intentions for the future. It's a time to celebrate the steps taken, both big and small, towards becoming our best selves.

Honoring Your Path and Embracing Your Evolution

1. Journaling Your Growth: Spend time writing about your experiences over the past year. Reflect on moments of learning, overcoming challenges, and personal victories.
2. Creating a Growth Collage: Make a visual representation of your growth using photos, quotes, or drawings that symbolize your journey this year.
3. Sharing Your Experiences: Consider sharing your reflections with a trusted friend or family member. Discussing your growth can offer new insights and perspectives.
4. Gratitude Practice: Acknowledge the people, experiences, and personal attributes you are grateful for that contributed to your growth this year.

Contemplating the Depth of Your Personal Journey

In what ways have I grown or changed this year?
Reflect on your emotional, mental, physical, and spiritual growth.

How can I apply the lessons learned this year to my future goals and aspirations?
Consider how your experiences this year can inform and inspire your path forward.

Weekly Goal

Your goal for this week is to engage in reflective practices that honor your personal growth. Recognize and celebrate your journey, acknowledging the strength and resilience you've shown throughout the year.

WEEK 52: SETTING INTENTIONS FOR THE FUTURE

date:

Looking Forward with Hope and Clarity

Welcome to Week 52, the final week of our self-care calendar. This week is about setting intentions for the future. As we close this chapter, it's an opportune time to look ahead and think about what we want to carry forward. <u>Setting intentions is a powerful way to focus our energy and align our actions with our values and goals.</u> It's about envisioning the life we want to lead and taking mindful steps towards it.

Crafting a Vision for the Future

1. <u>Vision Board Creation:</u> Create a vision board that represents your hopes, dreams, and goals for the future. Use images, words, and symbols that resonate with your aspirations.
2. <u>Writing a Letter to Your Future Self:</u> Write a letter to yourself, to be opened one year from now. Include your hopes, intentions, and encouragements.
3. <u>Meditation on Intentions:</u> Spend time in meditation, visualizing your intentions and imagining yourself living out these aspirations.
4. <u>Commitment to Action:</u> Identify one or two small steps you can take immediately towards your intentions. It's important to turn vision into action.

Envisioning the Path Ahead

What are my main goals and intentions for the coming year?
Define clear and meaningful objectives that align with your values and desires.

How can I stay aligned with my intentions throughout the year?
Think about strategies to keep your goals in focus, such as regular check-ins or journaling.

Weekly Goal

Set a goal to establish clear intentions for the coming year. Commit to taking small steps that align with these intentions, fostering a future filled with growth, fulfillment, and joy.

As you engage in these final weeks of self-care, remember that your journey is ongoing, filled with endless opportunities for growth and fulfillment. Embrace the lessons of the past and the possibilities of the future with an open heart and a hopeful spirit. Let the closing of this year be a stepping stone to a future where you continue to nurture, grow, and thrive.

Notes:

Notes:

Notes:

Notes:

Notes:

Notes:

Notes:

Notes:

Notes:

Notes:

Made in the USA
Monee, IL
09 December 2023

48583269R00066